The Limitless Mindset

The Limitless Mindset

Matthew Petchinsky

The Limitless Mindset: Unlock Your Untapped Potential

By: Matthew Petchinsky

Introduction
How Limiting Beliefs Hold You Back

Imagine standing at the edge of a vast ocean, ready to embark on a journey to discover distant lands filled with treasures and opportunities. Now, imagine that the only thing preventing you from setting sail is an anchor weighing down your ship. This anchor represents your limiting beliefs—those deeply rooted convictions that whisper doubts into your mind, convincing you that you're not smart enough, talented enough, or deserving enough to reach your goals.

Limiting beliefs are insidious. They often go unnoticed because they disguise themselves as "facts," reinforced by past experiences, societal expectations, or even well-meaning advice from loved ones. You might believe you're too old to start a new career, too young to be taken seriously, or too ordinary to make an extraordinary impact. These beliefs create invisible barriers that box you in, keeping you from stepping into your full potential.

But here's the truth: limiting beliefs are not truths. They are stories you've told yourself or inherited from others. And like any story, they can be rewritten. Yet, so many people remain trapped in the narratives of their limitations, afraid to question them or push beyond their comfort zones. The consequences of these self-imposed barriers are staggering. They not only restrict your personal growth but also rob the world of the unique gifts only you can offer.

Why Unlocking Potential Is Easier Than You Think

If limiting beliefs are the anchor, then unlocking your potential is the wind that propels your ship forward. The idea of reaching your potential might feel daunting, as if it requires Herculean effort or some mystical power you don't yet possess. But what if I told you that unlocking your potential is not about transforming into someone you're not? Instead, it's about recognizing and embracing the extraordinary within you.

The first step in this journey is understanding that you already have everything you need to succeed. Think of your potential as a seed planted deep within your soul. Just as a seed contains all the information it needs to grow into a towering tree, you possess the innate ability to grow, evolve, and achieve your dreams. The key lies in nurturing that seed by removing the weeds of doubt, fear, and hesitation that choke its growth.

Unlocking your potential begins with small, manageable shifts. It's about taking that first courageous step, however small, and then the next, and the next. It's not about perfection or grand gestures but about progress and persistence. The process becomes easier as you build momentum because each step forward fuels your confidence and reinforces your belief in what's possible.

Furthermore, unlocking your potential doesn't require you to reinvent the wheel. The tools, strategies, and mindsets you need are readily available. Whether it's through learning from others who have overcome similar challenges, adopting simple yet effective habits, or reprogramming your mind to see opportunities instead of obstacles, the path to your greatest self is more accessible than you think.

By shedding your limiting beliefs and embracing the truth of your limitless potential, you open doors to opportunities you never imagined possible. You begin to see challenges as stepping stones, failures as lessons, and dreams as destinations well within your reach. Most importantly, you transform not just your life but also the lives of those around you, inspiring them to embark on their own journeys of growth and self-discovery.

This book is your compass for that journey. It will guide you through the process of identifying and dismantling the beliefs holding you back, while equipping you with the tools to unlock your full potential. By the time you reach the final chapter, you'll not only believe in the extraordinary power within you—you'll be living it.

The time to lift the anchor and set sail is now. Are you ready to explore the vast ocean of your potential? Let's begin.

Chapter 1: Identifying Your Mental Blocks
Recognizing Internal Limitations

The human mind is a powerful tool, capable of shaping your reality and determining the course of your life. Yet, this same mind often becomes its own worst enemy. Internal limitations, also known as mental blocks, are the invisible barriers that prevent you from achieving your goals, reaching your potential, and living a fulfilled life. Recognizing these mental blocks is the first and most crucial step in dismantling them.

Internal limitations often manifest as thoughts, emotions, or behaviors that subtly (or overtly) sabotage your progress. They can take many forms, including:

1. **Self-Doubt**

   That little voice that says, *"I'm not good enough"* or *"What if I fail?"* Self-doubt often stems from past failures or fear of judgment and creates a cycle of hesitation and inaction.

2. **Fear of Failure or Success**

   Fear of failure is a common mental block, but fear of success is equally debilitating. Success often comes with change, responsibility, and heightened expectations, which can feel overwhelming.

3. **Perfectionism**

   The belief that everything must be perfect before you can proceed often paralyzes progress. Perfectionism creates unrealistic standards and prevents you from taking action, fearing you'll fall short.

4. **Negative Self-Talk**

   Your inner dialogue has immense power. Phrases like *"I can't do this"* or *"This is impossible"* can program your mind to accept defeat before you even begin.

5. **Limiting Beliefs**

Deeply ingrained beliefs about what you can or cannot achieve act as self-fulfilling prophecies. For example, believing *"I'm not smart enough to succeed"* or *"People like me don't achieve greatness"* keeps you stuck in a loop of limitation.

To recognize your mental blocks, start by observing your thoughts, emotions, and behaviors. Keep a journal to track recurring patterns of doubt, fear, or resistance. Pay attention to moments when you feel stuck, unmotivated, or overwhelmed. These are often indicators of an underlying mental block.

Ask yourself probing questions to uncover the root causes of your limitations:

- What beliefs do I hold about myself that might not be true?
- When have I held back from pursuing an opportunity, and why?
- What do I fear the most about stepping outside my comfort zone?

By shining a light on your internal limitations, you begin the process of reclaiming control over your mind and your life.

How to Challenge and Rewrite Negative Beliefs

Once you've identified your mental blocks, the next step is to challenge and rewrite them. This process involves reframing your perspective, questioning the validity of your beliefs, and replacing negative thought patterns with empowering ones.

1. **Question the Source of Your Beliefs**

    Every belief has an origin. Ask yourself:
    - Where did this belief come from?
    - Is it based on facts or assumptions?
    - Does this belief serve me or limit me?

For example, if you believe, *"I'll never be successful because I'm not naturally talented,"* consider where this belief originated. Did someone tell you this? Did a past failure reinforce it? Often, you'll find that limiting beliefs are based on outdated or inaccurate information.

2.Reframe Negative Thoughts

Reframing involves shifting your perspective to see a belief or situation in a more empowering light. Instead of thinking, *"I can't do this,"* replace it with, *"I may not know how to do this yet, but I'm capable of learning."*

Practice reframing by turning each limiting belief into a positive or neutral statement. For example:

-
    - Limiting belief: *"I always mess things up."*
    - Reframed belief: *"Mistakes are part of learning, and I grow from every experience."*

3.Gather Evidence Against Negative Beliefs

Your brain often seeks evidence to confirm your beliefs, a phenomenon known as confirmation bias. Counteract this by actively gathering evidence that disproves your negative beliefs.

- If you believe you're not good at public speaking, recall instances when you successfully communicated or received positive feedback.
- Write down your strengths and past achievements to remind yourself of your capabilities.

3.Use Affirmations and Visualization

Affirmations are positive statements that help reprogram your subconscious mind. Repeat affirmations daily to reinforce empowering beliefs. For example:

- *"I am capable of achieving my goals."*
- *"I have the skills and determination to succeed."*

Pair affirmations with visualization exercises. Imagine yourself overcoming challenges, achieving your goals, and living the life you desire. Visualization helps create a mental blueprint for success, making it easier to take action.

1. **Take Action Despite Fear**
   One of the most effective ways to dismantle a mental block is to take action, even when it feels uncomfortable. Fear loses its power when you confront it head-on. Start small and gradually push your boundaries. Each step forward builds confidence and weakens the grip of your limiting beliefs.
2. **Seek Support and Accountability**
   Share your journey with trusted friends, mentors, or a coach who can provide encouragement and hold you accountable. Sometimes, an outside perspective can help you see your potential more clearly and challenge beliefs you've accepted as truth.
3. **Celebrate Progress, Not Perfection**
   Remember that growth is a journey, not a destination. Celebrate small wins along the way, and don't let setbacks discourage you. Each step forward, no matter how small, is a victory over your mental blocks.

The Power of a Transformed Mind

As you challenge and rewrite your negative beliefs, you'll notice a shift in your mindset, confidence, and actions. You'll begin to see opportunities where you once saw obstacles and possibilities where you once saw limitations. The process of identifying and overcoming mental blocks is transformative, allowing you to unlock your potential and step into a life of greater freedom, fulfillment, and success.

This chapter is your starting point. By recognizing internal limitations and actively challenging them, you lay the foundation for a life unbound by fear, doubt, or hesitation. The journey may not always be easy, but it will always be worth it. The next step is yours to take. Are you ready?

Chapter 2: Cultivating a Growth Mindset
Shifting from Fixed to Expansive Thinking

At the heart of personal and professional growth lies a fundamental concept: your mindset. A growth mindset, a term popularized by psychologist Carol Dweck, is the belief that your abilities, intelligence, and talents can be developed through effort, learning, and persistence. It stands in stark contrast to a fixed mindset, which views these traits as static and unchangeable.

To cultivate a growth mindset, the first step is to identify and challenge fixed thinking patterns that limit your progress.

Characteristics of a Fixed Mindset:

- Avoiding challenges for fear of failure.
- Viewing effort as a sign of inadequacy rather than a path to mastery.
- Believing that success is based on innate talent rather than hard work.
- Feeling threatened by others' achievements.

Characteristics of a Growth Mindset:

- Embracing challenges as opportunities to grow.
- Viewing effort as essential to success.
- Understanding that failure is a stepping stone to improvement.
- Drawing inspiration from others' successes.

How to Shift to Expansive Thinking:

1. **Recognize Fixed Mindset Triggers**
   Fixed mindset thoughts often arise in moments of stress, failure, or uncertainty. For example, if you face a challenging task, you might think, *"I'm just not good at this, so there's no point in trying."* Recognizing these triggers allows you to pause and redirect your thoughts.

2. **Adopt a "Not Yet" Mentality**
   Instead of saying, *"I can't do this,"* say, *"I can't do this yet."* This small shift opens the door to possibility and emphasizes the potential for growth over time.

3. **Reframe Setbacks as Learning Experiences**
   When something doesn't go as planned, ask yourself:
   - *What can I learn from this?*
   - *How can I do better next time?*
     Treat failures not as evidence of inadequacy but as valuable feedback on your journey to mastery.

4. **Surround Yourself with Growth-Oriented Influences**
   Engage with people, books, podcasts, or other resources that promote a growth mindset. Surrounding yourself with positivity and inspiration will reinforce your commitment to expansive thinking.

5. **Practice Gratitude for Progress**
   Celebrate your growth, no matter how small. Reflect on where you started and how far you've come. This practice builds momentum and reinforces the belief that effort leads to improvement.

Shifting from fixed to expansive thinking is a process that requires intention and persistence. Over time, you'll notice your mindset becoming more adaptable, optimistic, and resilient in the face of challenges.

How to Embrace Challenges as Opportunities

One of the defining traits of a growth mindset is the ability to see challenges not as obstacles but as opportunities for growth. Embracing challenges requires a fundamental shift in how you perceive discomfort, risk, and failure.

1. Change Your Relationship with Discomfort

Growth often lies just beyond your comfort zone. Challenges naturally bring discomfort, but this discomfort is a sign that you're stretching yourself. Instead of avoiding it, lean into it with curiosity and a willingness to learn.

2. Reframe Challenges as Experiments

View challenges as experiments where the outcome is valuable regardless of success or failure. By shifting your focus to the process of exploration and discovery, you remove the pressure of perfection and create space for innovation.

For example, if you're launching a new project, focus on what you can learn from the experience rather than fixating on achieving immediate success.

3. Break Challenges into Manageable Steps

Overwhelming challenges can feel insurmountable. Break them down into smaller, actionable steps. Each step completed builds confidence and creates a sense of accomplishment, making the overall challenge more approachable.

4. Use a "What If" Mindset

When faced with a challenge, ask yourself empowering "what if" questions:

- *What if this works out better than I imagined?*
- *What if I discover a new strength or skill in the process?*
- *What if I grow stronger, smarter, or more capable because of this?*

These questions shift your focus from fear of failure to the potential rewards of the experience.

5. Develop Resilience Through Reflection

After facing a challenge, take time to reflect on the experience:

- *What did I learn about myself?*
- *What skills or strengths did I develop?*
- *How can I apply these lessons moving forward?*

Reflection turns challenges into valuable life lessons and builds resilience for future obstacles.

6. Find the Opportunity in Every Challenge

Even in the most difficult situations, there is often a hidden opportunity. Perhaps a failed business venture teaches you critical lessons for your next endeavor, or a difficult relationship helps you develop greater emotional intelligence.

To find these opportunities, ask yourself:

- *How can I grow from this experience?*
- *What skills or knowledge can I gain?*
- *How might this challenge lead to something better?*

7. Leverage Support Systems

Facing challenges doesn't mean you have to go it alone. Seek guidance, mentorship, or collaboration from others who can provide perspective and encouragement. Sharing your struggles and learning from others can transform challenges into shared growth experiences.

The Ripple Effect of a Growth Mindset

Cultivating a growth mindset doesn't just benefit you; it also impacts the people around you. When you embrace challenges with enthusiasm and resilience, you inspire others to do the same. Your growth mindset becomes a beacon of possibility, showing others that they, too, can achieve their goals through effort and determination.

By shifting from fixed to expansive thinking and learning to embrace challenges as opportunities, you unlock a powerful tool for personal and professional transformation. A growth mindset is not a destination but a way of life—one that allows you to continuously evolve, adapt, and thrive no matter what obstacles come your way.

Chapter 3: Leveraging Visualization
Using Mental Imagery to Fuel Success

Visualization is one of the most powerful tools for achieving success. By creating vivid mental images of your desired outcomes, you can align your thoughts, emotions, and actions toward achieving your goals. The science behind visualization is rooted in the brain's ability to simulate experiences. When you visualize, your brain activates the same neural pathways as if you were physically performing the task. This not only boosts confidence but also enhances your ability to succeed.

The Science of Visualization

1. **Mental Rehearsal and Neural Pathways**

   Studies show that mental rehearsal activates the brain's motor cortex, which is responsible for planning and executing physical movements. For example, athletes who visualize themselves practicing their sport show measurable improvements in performance, even without physical practice.

2. **The Reticular Activating System (RAS)**

   The RAS is a network of neurons in your brainstem that filters information based on what you focus on. When you visualize a goal, your RAS helps you notice opportunities, resources, and connections aligned with that vision, making it easier to move toward your objectives.

3. **Emotional Resonance**

   Visualization allows you to experience the emotions associated with success before it happens. Feeling the joy, pride, or excitement of achieving your goal motivates you to take action and persist through challenges.

Practical Benefits of Visualization

- **Clarity**: Visualization helps you define what success looks and feels like, making your goals more tangible and specific.
- **Motivation**: Seeing yourself achieve your goals energizes you and keeps you focused on what matters most.
- **Resilience**: Mental imagery reinforces your belief in your ability to overcome obstacles, reducing self-doubt and fear of failure.

Techniques to Visualize Success

1. **Create a Clear Picture of Your Goal**
   Be as specific as possible about what you want to achieve. Instead of visualizing "success," imagine yourself reaching a specific milestone, such as landing your dream job, completing a marathon, or giving a successful presentation.

Example: If your goal is to write a bestselling book, visualize the book cover, the title, and your name in bold print. Imagine readers praising your work and see the book on bestseller lists.

Engage All Your Senses

Make your visualization as vivid and immersive as possible by incorporating all five senses:

- **Sight**: What does your goal look like?
- **Sound**: What sounds accompany your success? Applause? Laughter? Encouraging words?
- **Smell**: Are there specific scents, like the aroma of fresh ink on a published book?
- **Touch**: How does success feel physically? A firm handshake? The texture of a medal?
- **Taste**: Is there a celebratory meal or drink involved?

2. **Visualize the Process, Not Just the Outcome**

   While imagining the end result is motivating, it's equally important to visualize the steps required to get there. See yourself working hard, solving problems, and staying committed to your goal. This reinforces the belief that success comes from consistent effort.

3. **Practice Regularly**

   Set aside time each day to practice visualization. It can be as short as 5–10 minutes in the morning or before bed. Consistency is key to programming your mind for success.

Techniques to Program Your Subconscious for Growth

Visualization is not just about seeing; it's about creating lasting change in your subconscious mind. Your subconscious controls many of your behaviors, habits, and beliefs. By programming it for growth, you align your actions with your goals on a deeper level.

1. Combine Visualization with Affirmations

Pair your mental imagery with positive affirmations that reinforce your goals. For example, if you're visualizing a successful presentation, repeat affirmations like:

- *"I am confident and prepared."*
- *"My ideas resonate with my audience."*

Repeating these affirmations during visualization creates a strong connection between your goals and your belief in achieving them.

2. Use Emotional Anchors

Attach powerful emotions to your visualizations. Feel the pride, gratitude, and joy of achieving your goal as if it has already happened. These emotions act as anchors, making your subconscious more receptive to your vision.

3. Leverage the "Act As If" Principle

Visualize yourself not only achieving your goals but also embodying the person you want to become. Imagine how you would think, speak, and act as the future version of yourself. For instance:

- If you aspire to be a successful entrepreneur, see yourself confidently making decisions, networking with influential people, and celebrating milestones.
- Act "as if" in your daily life by adopting the habits and behaviors of that future self.

4. Create a Vision Board

A vision board is a tangible tool that reinforces your visualization practice. Fill it with images, quotes, and symbols that represent your goals. Place it somewhere you'll see daily to keep your aspirations top of mind.

5. Incorporate Guided Visualization Exercises

Guided visualization exercises, available through apps, podcasts, or videos, can help you focus and refine your practice. These exercises often combine visualization with relaxation techniques, making it easier to access your subconscious mind.

6. Use Sleep to Your Advantage

Your subconscious mind is most receptive during the moments before sleep and immediately upon waking. Use this time to visualize your goals and repeat affirmations, allowing your subconscious to absorb these positive messages overnight.

7. Practice Gratitude Visualization

Spend time visualizing things you're grateful for. Gratitude fosters a positive mindset and reinforces the belief that more good things are possible. As you visualize success, feel gratitude for the opportunities, resources, and progress you already have.

Overcoming Common Challenges in Visualization

1. **Difficulty Staying Focused**

   If your mind tends to wander, start with shorter visualization sessions and gradually increase their duration. Guided exercises can also help maintain focus.

2. **Struggling to Create Vivid Images**

   If you find it hard to visualize clearly, focus on the emotions and general sensations of success rather than the details. Over time, your ability to create vivid mental images will improve.

3. **Doubts and Negative Thoughts**

   It's normal for doubts to arise during visualization. Instead of resisting them, acknowledge their presence and gently redirect your focus to your desired outcome.

The Transformative Power of Visualization

When practiced consistently, visualization can transform your mindset, behaviors, and results. It bridges the gap between where you are and where you want to be by programming your subconscious to act in alignment with your goals.

Visualization is not magic, but its effects often feel magical. It amplifies your focus, strengthens your determination, and enhances your ability to navigate challenges. Most importantly, it helps you build the mental foundation for success, ensuring that your journey is not only possible but also enjoyable.

Now that you understand how to leverage visualization, it's time to integrate this powerful practice into your daily routine.

Chapter 4: Building Momentum Through Action

Momentum is the force that transforms your aspirations into achievements. While visualization and planning are essential, progress ultimately requires action. However, taking action often feels daunting, especially when faced with the enormity of a long-term goal. This chapter focuses on how starting small can lead to significant results and how to overcome the inertia of procrastination to build lasting momentum.

Starting Small to Achieve Big Results

Large goals can feel overwhelming, like standing at the base of a mountain and looking up at its peak. The secret to scaling that mountain lies in breaking the journey into small, manageable steps.

1. The Power of Micro-Action

Micro-actions are tiny, easily achievable tasks that move you closer to your goal. These actions might seem insignificant, but they build momentum by creating a sense of accomplishment and progress. For example:

- Instead of writing an entire book chapter in one sitting, aim to write 200 words per day.
- If your goal is to exercise regularly, start with a 5-minute workout.

Each micro-action reinforces a habit of consistency, which is more important than intensity when building momentum.

2. The Domino Effect

Small wins have a compounding effect. When you complete one task, it creates a ripple of motivation and confidence, making it easier to tackle the next. This is known as the domino effect. A single small action, like organizing your workspace, can trigger a series of productive behaviors that lead to significant outcomes.

3. Setting Achievable Milestones

Break your larger goal into smaller milestones that are specific, measurable, and time-bound. For example:

- If your goal is to lose 30 pounds, set a milestone to lose 5 pounds within the first month.
- If you're launching a business, start by creating a one-page business plan before diving into a full-scale strategy.

Celebrate each milestone as a victory. This recognition reinforces your belief in your ability to achieve bigger results.

4. Consistency Over Perfection

Focus on consistency rather than perfection. Even small, imperfect actions taken consistently will yield better results than waiting for the perfect moment or execution. Remember: progress, not perfection, is the goal.

Breaking Through Procrastination

Procrastination is the enemy of momentum. It keeps you stuck in a cycle of inaction, driven by fear, overwhelm, or a lack of clarity. Breaking free from procrastination requires understanding its root causes and implementing practical strategies to overcome it.

1. Understand Why You Procrastinate

Procrastination often stems from one or more of the following:

- **Fear of Failure**: Avoiding action to escape the possibility of making mistakes.
- **Overwhelm**: Feeling paralyzed by the size or complexity of a task.
- **Perfectionism**: Waiting for ideal conditions or flawless execution.
- **Lack of Clarity**: Not knowing where or how to start.

Identify the specific reason behind your procrastination. This self-awareness is the first step in overcoming it.

2. Use the "Two-Minute Rule"

The two-minute rule states: If a task takes less than two minutes, do it immediately. For larger tasks, break them into steps that can be started in under two minutes. For example:

- If you're procrastinating on a report, open a blank document and write the title.
- If you're avoiding exercise, put on your workout clothes.

Taking even the smallest action reduces resistance and makes it easier to keep going.

3. Prioritize Tasks with the Eisenhower Matrix

The Eisenhower Matrix helps you prioritize tasks based on their urgency and importance:

- **Urgent and Important**: Do these tasks immediately.
- **Important but Not Urgent**: Schedule these tasks.
- **Urgent but Not Important**: Delegate these tasks if possible.
- **Neither Urgent nor Important**: Eliminate these tasks to free up time and energy.

Organizing tasks in this way reduces overwhelm and ensures you focus on what truly matters.

4. Overcome Perfectionism

Perfectionism often leads to procrastination because the fear of not meeting high standards prevents you from starting. Combat perfectionism by:

- Setting realistic expectations.
- Focusing on progress rather than flawless execution.
- Giving yourself permission to produce a "first draft" or "rough version."

Remember, you can always improve and refine your work later.

5. Time-Blocking and Scheduling

Schedule specific blocks of time for focused work on your tasks. Treat these time blocks as non-negotiable appointments with yourself. For example:

- Allocate 30 minutes in the morning to work on your most important task.
- Dedicate 15 minutes in the evening to review your progress and plan for the next day.

Time-blocking creates structure and eliminates decision fatigue, making it easier to take action.

6. Leverage Accountability

Accountability is a powerful motivator. Share your goals with a trusted friend, mentor, or coach who can hold you accountable for taking action. Alternatively, join a group or community of like-minded individuals working toward similar goals.

7. Reward Yourself for Taking Action

Create a system of rewards to reinforce positive behavior. For example:

- Treat yourself to a favorite snack or activity after completing a challenging task.
- Plan a larger reward, like a weekend getaway, for achieving a major milestone.

Rewards create a positive association with taking action, making it easier to stay motivated.

The Momentum Multiplier

Once you've taken the first steps to overcome procrastination and start small, you'll notice an increase in energy and motivation. This is the momentum multiplier at work. To maintain this momentum:

1. **Track Your Progress**

   Use a journal, app, or tracker to log your daily actions and milestones. Seeing tangible evidence of your progress reinforces your commitment and keeps you motivated.

2. **Review and Adjust Regularly**

   Periodically review your goals and strategies. Adjust your approach as needed to stay aligned with your objectives and maintain momentum.

3. **Stay Flexible and Resilient**

   Understand that setbacks are a natural part of the process. Instead of letting them derail your progress, use them as opportunities to learn and grow. Resilience is key to sustaining momentum over the long term.

4. **Build Positive Habits**

   Incorporate habits that support your goals into your daily routine. For example:
   - Start each day with a morning ritual that includes goal-setting and visualization.
   - Dedicate time each week to reflect on your accomplishments and plan for the week ahead.

Building a Life of Action

Momentum is the bridge between intention and achievement. By starting small, breaking through procrastination, and sustaining consistent action, you set yourself on a path to success. Each step you take builds confidence, capability, and clarity, propelling you closer to your goals.

As you embrace the power of momentum, remember that the journey itself is as valuable as the destination. Celebrate every step forward, and trust that consistent action will create the life you envision.

Chapter 5: Sustaining the Limitless Mindset

A limitless mindset isn't achieved overnight—it's cultivated through intentional daily habits and a commitment to lifelong growth. Once you've begun unlocking your potential, the next challenge is maintaining the mindset that allows you to continue thriving. This chapter explores the habits and tools that will help you sustain a limitless mindset and build a life of continuous improvement.

Daily Habits to Nurture Your Full Potential

The habits you cultivate shape your thoughts, emotions, and actions. By embedding the following practices into your daily routine, you can consistently nurture your limitless mindset.

1. Start Your Day with Intention

How you begin your day sets the tone for everything that follows. Start with a morning routine that aligns your mind and body with your goals:

- **Gratitude Practice**: Spend a few minutes reflecting on what you're grateful for. Gratitude shifts your focus from limitations to abundance and sets a positive tone.
- **Visualization and Affirmations**: Visualize your goals and repeat empowering affirmations to prime your mind for success. For example:
    - *"I am capable of overcoming any challenge."*
    - *"Today, I will take one step closer to my dreams."*
- **Movement**: Incorporate physical activity to energize your body and mind. This could be stretching, yoga, or a brisk walk.

2. Cultivate Self-Awareness

Self-awareness is the foundation of growth. Develop a habit of checking in with yourself throughout the day:

- Ask reflective questions like:
    - *"Am I acting in alignment with my goals?"*
    - *"What emotions am I experiencing, and why?"*
- Practice mindfulness by focusing on the present moment without judgment. Use techniques like deep breathing or meditation to center yourself.

3. Embrace Continuous Learning

A limitless mindset thrives on knowledge and curiosity. Make learning a daily priority:

- Dedicate time to reading books, articles, or listening to podcasts that challenge and inspire you.
- Explore new skills or hobbies to keep your mind engaged and adaptable.
- Reflect on lessons learned from daily experiences, whether successes or setbacks.

4. Take Decisive Action

Action reinforces belief. Commit to taking at least one meaningful step toward your goals every day, no matter how small. Consistent action builds momentum and strengthens your sense of capability.

5. Surround Yourself with Positivity

Your environment plays a significant role in shaping your mindset:

- Engage with people who uplift and challenge you to grow.
- Limit exposure to negativity, whether from toxic relationships, media, or self-talk.

- Create a physical space that inspires productivity and creativity, such as a clutter-free desk or a vision board.

6. Celebrate Progress, Not Just Outcomes

Acknowledge and celebrate your wins, no matter how small. This practice reinforces your motivation and helps you focus on the journey rather than fixating solely on the destination.

Tools for Lifelong Personal Growth

A limitless mindset requires the right tools to stay adaptable, resilient, and focused. The following resources and strategies will help you maintain your commitment to personal growth over the long term.

1. Journaling

Journaling is a powerful tool for self-reflection and clarity:

- **Daily Gratitude Journal**: Write down three things you're grateful for each day to cultivate a positive outlook.
- **Reflection Journal**: Reflect on challenges, successes, and lessons learned.
- **Goal-Tracking Journal**: Record your goals, milestones, and progress to stay accountable.

2. Time Management Systems

Effective time management ensures that you're consistently working toward your goals:

- **The Pomodoro Technique**: Break work into focused intervals (e.g., 25 minutes of work followed by a 5-minute break) to maintain productivity and prevent burnout.
- **The Eisenhower Matrix**: Prioritize tasks based on urgency and importance to focus on what truly matters.
- **Habit Trackers**: Use apps or planners to track daily habits and reinforce consistency.

3. Mindfulness and Meditation Apps

Mindfulness strengthens your focus and emotional resilience:

- Apps like **Headspace**, **Calm**, or **Insight Timer** offer guided meditations and mindfulness exercises.
- Practice mindful breathing for a few minutes each day to reduce stress and improve clarity.

4. Learning Platforms and Resources

Stay curious and continue expanding your knowledge:

- Platforms like **Coursera**, **Udemy**, or **MasterClass** offer courses on a wide range of topics.
- Join book clubs or discussion groups to engage with new ideas and perspectives.

5. Accountability and Mentorship

Building relationships with supportive individuals can accelerate your growth:

- Join communities or masterminds with like-minded individuals who share your goals.
- Seek mentorship from someone who has achieved what you aspire to accomplish.
- Consider hiring a coach to provide personalized guidance and accountability.

6. Technology for Goal Setting and Tracking

Leverage technology to streamline your progress:

- Use apps like **Trello**, **Asana**, or **Notion** to organize tasks and track goals.
- Set reminders and alerts to ensure you stay consistent with daily habits.
- Explore tools like **Habitica**, which gamifies habit-building for added motivation.

7. Regular Reflection and Growth Audits

Schedule periodic "growth audits" to assess your progress:

- Reflect on what's working, what's not, and where you can improve.
- Adjust your strategies and goals based on new insights and circumstances.
- Celebrate accomplishments to reinforce your commitment to growth.

Overcoming Challenges to Sustaining a Limitless Mindset

Even with the best intentions, life's challenges can test your commitment to a limitless mindset. Here's how to navigate common obstacles:

1. Dealing with Setbacks

Setbacks are inevitable but don't have to derail your progress. When faced with failure:

- Reframe the experience as a learning opportunity.
- Ask yourself: *"What can I do differently next time?"*
- Seek support from mentors or peers who can provide perspective and encouragement.

2. Battling Self-Doubt

Self-doubt can creep in, especially during periods of uncertainty. Combat it by:

- Revisiting your achievements to remind yourself of your capabilities.
- Using affirmations and visualization to rebuild confidence.
- Focusing on small wins to regain momentum.

3. Managing Burnout

Overcommitting can lead to exhaustion and burnout. Protect your energy by:

- Scheduling regular breaks and time for self-care.
- Setting boundaries to avoid overextending yourself.
- Delegating or eliminating non-essential tasks to prioritize what matters most.

A Life of Limitless Possibilities

Sustaining a limitless mindset is not about perfection but persistence. By cultivating daily habits that support your growth and leveraging tools to stay focused, you create a life where possibilities are endless. The journey of personal growth is lifelong, filled with opportunities to learn, adapt, and evolve.

Every day presents a new chance to nurture your full potential, break through barriers, and expand your horizons. With the right mindset, habits, and tools, you'll not only achieve your goals but also discover the joy and fulfillment of living a limitless life.

Appendix A: Exercises for Breaking Mental Barriers

Breaking through mental barriers is essential for personal growth and achieving your goals. This appendix provides actionable exercises designed to identify, challenge, and overcome limiting beliefs, self-doubt, and other mental obstacles. These exercises are practical, easy to implement, and can be adapted to suit your unique needs.

1. The Limiting Belief Excavation Exercise

This exercise helps uncover and dismantle deep-seated limiting beliefs.

Steps:

1. **Identify a Specific Limiting Belief**

   Write down one belief that you feel is holding you back. For example:
   - *"I'm not good enough to lead a team."*
   - *"I'll never be financially secure."*

2. **Examine the Origin**

   Reflect on where this belief came from. Ask yourself:
   - *When did I first start believing this?*
   - *Did someone else impose this belief on me?*
   - *Is this belief based on facts or assumptions?*

3. **Challenge the Belief**

   Write down evidence that contradicts the belief. For example:
   - Times when you successfully led a group or managed a task.
   - Achievements that demonstrate your capability.

4. **Reframe the Belief**

   Replace the limiting belief with an empowering one. For example:

- ◦ Instead of *"I'm not good enough to lead a team,"* write: *"I am capable of leading with confidence and learning as I grow."*

5. **Reinforce the New Belief**

Repeat the new belief daily as an affirmation. Visualize scenarios where you embody this belief.

2. The Fear-Facing Framework

This exercise addresses fears that create mental barriers, helping you take action despite them.

Steps:

1. **Name Your Fear**

   Write down the specific fear holding you back. For example:
   - *"I'm afraid of public speaking because I might embarrass myself."*

2. **Explore the Worst-Case Scenario**

   Imagine the worst possible outcome of facing this fear. Ask yourself:
   - *What's the absolute worst that could happen?*
   - *How likely is this to occur?*

3. **Create a Contingency Plan**

   Identify steps you could take to recover if the worst-case scenario happens. For example:
   - If you forget your lines during a presentation, plan to have cue cards or notes handy.

4. **Focus on the Best-Case Scenario**

   Visualize the best possible outcome. Ask yourself:
   - *What opportunities could arise if I overcome this fear?*
   - *How will I feel once I succeed?*

5. **Take Incremental Action**

   Start with small, low-stakes actions to build confidence. For example:
   - Practice speaking in front of a mirror or a trusted friend before presenting to a larger audience.

3. The Visualization Reset Exercise

Use this exercise to reprogram your mind and overcome mental barriers by visualizing success.

Steps:

1. **Set the Scene**

   Choose a quiet, comfortable place where you won't be disturbed. Close your eyes and take a few deep breaths to relax.

2. **Identify the Barrier**

   Visualize the mental barrier you want to overcome. For example:
   - A feeling of inadequacy in your career.

3. **Replace the Barrier with Success**

   Picture yourself succeeding in the area where the barrier exists. Make the visualization vivid by engaging all your senses:
   - What does success look like?
   - How does it feel emotionally and physically?
   - What sounds or words accompany the moment?

4. **Anchor the Feeling**

   While visualizing, place your hand over your heart or clench your fist to create a physical anchor for the feeling of success.

5. **Repeat Daily**

   Practice this visualization for 5–10 minutes each day to reinforce the belief that you can overcome the barrier.

4. The Self-Talk Reframe

Negative self-talk often reinforces mental barriers. This exercise helps you identify and replace unhelpful inner dialogue.

Steps:

1. **Track Your Self-Talk**

   For one day, jot down any negative thoughts or self-criticisms you notice. For example:
   - *"I'm terrible at this."*
   - *"I'll never figure this out."*

2. **Identify Patterns**

   Review your notes and look for recurring themes. These patterns often point to deeper mental barriers.

3. **Challenge Each Thought**

   For each negative thought, ask yourself:
   - *Is this true?*
   - *What evidence supports or contradicts this thought?*

4. **Rewrite the Thought**

   Transform the negative thought into a positive or neutral statement. For example:
   - Replace *"I'm terrible at this"* with *"I'm learning and improving every day."*

5. **Practice Positive Affirmations**

   Create a list of affirmations to counteract negative self-talk. Repeat these affirmations daily, especially when the negative thoughts resurface.

5. The Comfort Zone Expansion Challenge

This exercise helps you break free from mental barriers by gradually expanding your comfort zone.

Steps:

1. **Define Your Comfort Zone**

   List activities or situations where you feel safe and comfortable. For example:
   - Sticking to familiar routines.
   - Avoiding public speaking or networking events.

2. **Identify a Stretch Goal**

   Choose a goal that pushes you slightly beyond your comfort zone but isn't overwhelming. For example:
   - Speaking up in a meeting or attending a networking event.

3. **Create a Step-by-Step Plan**

   Break the goal into smaller, manageable actions. For example:
   - Start by practicing your speaking points with a friend.
   - Attend a virtual networking event before attending one in person.

4. **Track Your Progress**

   Keep a journal of each step you take and how it feels. Celebrate your progress, no matter how small.

5. **Reflect and Repeat**

   After completing one challenge, reflect on what you learned and set a new stretch goal.

6. The Values Alignment Exercise

When your actions align with your core values, mental barriers lose their power. This exercise helps you identify and align with your values.

Steps:

1. **Identify Your Core Values**

   Write down the principles that matter most to you. For example:
   - Honesty, growth, creativity, or connection.

2. **Evaluate Your Barriers**

   Identify which mental barriers conflict with your values. For example:
   - If growth is a core value, fear of failure may be a barrier that prevents you from pursuing new opportunities.

3. **Align Your Actions**

   Choose actions that honor your values and challenge your barriers. For example:
   - If creativity is a value, start a project you've been procrastinating on.

4. **Reinforce Value-Driven Behavior**

   Reflect on how these actions align with your values and the impact they have on your mindset.

Conclusion

Breaking mental barriers requires intentional effort, but the rewards are transformative. These exercises are designed to help you identify, challenge, and replace limiting beliefs with empowering ones. By practicing them consistently, you'll not only overcome obstacles but also unlock new levels of potential and confidence.

Choose the exercises that resonate most with you, and integrate them into your routine. Over time, you'll notice a shift in your mindset and your ability to tackle challenges with resilience and determination. The path to a limitless mindset starts here—one exercise at a time.

<u>Message from the Author:</u>

I hope you enjoyed this book, I love astrology and knew there was not a book such as this out on the shelf. I love metaphysical items as well. Please check out my other books:

-Life of Government Benefits

-My life of Hell

-My life with Hydrocephalus

-Red Sky

-World Domination:Woman's rule

-World Domination:Woman's Rule 2: The War

-Life and Banishment of Apophis: book 1

-The Kidney Friendly Diet

-The Ultimate Hemp Cookbook

-Creating a Dispensary(legally)

-Cleanliness throughout life: the importance of showering from childhood to adulthood.

-Strong Roots: The Risks of Overcoddling children

-Hemp Horoscopes: Cosmic Insights and Earthly Healing

- Celestial Hemp Navigating the Zodiac: Through the Green Cosmos

-Astrological Hemp: Aligning The Stars with Earth's Ancient Herb

-The Astrological Guide to Hemp: Stars, Signs, and Sacred Leaves

-Green Growth: Innovative Marketing Strategies for your Hemp Products and Dispensary

-Cosmic Cannabis

-Astrological Munchies

-Henry The Hemp

-Zodiacal Roots: The Astrological Soul Of Hemp

- **Green Constellations: Intersection of Hemp and Zodiac**

-Hemp in The Houses: An astrological Adventure Through The Cannabis Galaxy

-Galactic Ganja Guide

Heavenly Hemp
Zodiac Leaves
Doctor Who Astrology
Cannastrology
Stellar Satvias and Cosmic Indicas
<u>Celestial Cannabis: A Zodiac Journey</u>
AstroHerbology: The Sky and The Soil: Volume 1
AstroHerbology:Celestial Cannabis:Volume 2
Cosmic Cannabis Cultivation
The Starry Guide to Herbal Harmony: Volume 1
The Starry Guide to Herbal Harmony: Cannabis Universe: Volume 2

Yugioh Astrology: Astrological Guide to Deck, Duels and more
Nightmare Mansion: Echoes of The Abyss
Nightmare Mansion 2: Legacy of Shadows
Nightmare Mansion 3: Shadows of the Forgotten
Nightmare Mansion 4: Echoes of the Damned
The Life and Banishment of Apophis: Book 2
Nightmare Mansion: Halls of Despair
<u>Healing with Herb: Cannabis and Hydrocephalus</u>
<u>Planetary Pot: Aligning with Astrological Herbs: Volume 1</u>
Fast Track to Freedom: 30 Days to Financial Independence Using AI, Assets, and Agile Hustles
<u>Cosmic Hemp Pathways</u>
How to Become Financially Free in 30 Days: 10,000 Paths to Prosperity
Zodiacal Herbage: Astrological Insights: Volume 1
Nightmare Mansion: Whispers in the Walls
The Daleks Invade Atlantis
Henry the hemp and Hydrocephalus

10X The Kidney Friendly Diet
Cannabis Universe: Adult coloring book

The Boogey Book

Locked In Reflection: A Chastity Journey Through Locktober

Generating Wealth Quickly:

How to Generate $100,000 in 24 Hours

Star Magic: Harness the Power of the Universe

The Flatulence Chronicles: A Fart Journal for Self-Discovery

The Doctor and The Death Moth

Seize the Day: A Personal Seizure Tracking Journal

The Ultimate Boogeyman Safari: A Journey into the Boogie World and Beyond

Whispers of Samhain: 1,000 Spells of Love, Luck, and Lunar Magic: Samhain Spell Book

Apophis's guides:

Witch's Spellbook Crafting Guide for Halloween

<u>Frost & Flame: The Enchanted Yule Grimoire of 1000 Winter Spells</u>

<u>The Ultimate Boogey Goo Guide & Spooky Activities for Halloween Fun</u>

Harmony of the Scales: A Libra's Spellcraft for Balance and Beauty

The Enchanted Advent: 36 Days of Christmas Wonders

Nightmare Mansion: The Labyrinth of Screams

Harvest of Enchantment: 1,000 Spells of Gratitude, Love, and Fortune for Thanksgiving

The Boogey Chronicles: A Journal of Nightly Encounters and Shadowy Secrets

The 12 Days of Financial Freedom: A Step-by-Step Christmas Countdown to Transform Your Finances

Sigil of the Eternal Spiral Blank Journal

A Christmas Feast: Timeless Recipes for Every Meal

Holiday Stress-Free Solutions: A Survival Guide to Thriving During the Festive Season

Whispers of the Harvest: The Corn Mother's Journal

The Evergreen Spellbook

The Doctor Meets the Boogeyman

The White Witch of Rose Hall's SpellBook

The Gingerbread Golem's Shadow: A Study in Sweet Darkness

The Gingerbread Golem Codex: An Academic Exploration of Sweet Myths

The Gingerbread Golem Grimoire: Sweet Magicks and Spells for the Festive Witch

The Curse of the Gingerbread Golem

10-minute Christmas Crafts for kids

<u>Christmas Crisis Solutions: The Ultimate Last-Minute Survival Guide</u>

Gingerbread Golem Recipes: Holiday Treats with a Magical Twist

The Infinite Key: Unlocking Mystical Secrets of the Ages

Enchanted Yule: A Wiccan and Pagan Guide to a Magical and Memorable Season

Dinosaurs of Power: Unlocking Ancient Magick

Astro-Dinos: The Cosmic Guide to Prehistoric Wisdom

Gallifrey's Yule Logs: A Festive Doctor Who Cookbook

The Dino Grimoire: Secrets of Prehistoric Magick

The Gift They Never Knew They Needed

The Gingerbread Golem's Culinary Alchemy: Enchanting Recipes for a Sweetly Dark Feast

A Time Lord Christmas: Holiday Adventures with the Doctor

Krampusproofing Your Home: Defensive Strategies for Yule

Silent Frights: A Collection of Christmas Crecpypastas to Chill Your Bones

Santa Raptor's Jolly Carnage: A Dino-Claus Christmas Tale

Prehistoric Palettes: A Dino Wicca Coloring Journey

The Christmas Wishkeeper Chronicles

The Starlight Sleigh: A Holiday Journey

Elf Secrets: The True Magic of the North Pole

Candy Cane Conjurations

Cooking with Kids: Recipes Under 20 Minutes

Doctor Who: The TARDIS Confiscation

The Anxiety First Aid Kit: Quick Tools to Calm Your Mind

Frosty Whispers: A Winter's Tale

The Infinite Key: Unlocking the Secrets to Prosperity, Resilience, and Purpose

The Grasping Void: Why You'll Regret This Purchase

Astrology for Busy Bees: Star Signs Simplified

The Instant Focus Formula: Cut Through the Noise

The Secret Language of Colors: Unlocking the Emotional Codes

Sacred Fossil Chronicles: Blank Journal

The Christmas Cottage Miracle

Feeding Frenzy: Graboid-Inspired Recipes

Manifest in Minutes: The Quick Law of Attraction Guide

The Symbiote Chronicles: Doctor Who's Venomous Journey

Think Tiny, Grow Big: The Minimalist Mindset

The Energy Key: Unlocking Limitless Motivation

New Year, New Magic: Manifesting Your Best Year Yet

Unstoppable You: Mastering Confidence in Minutes

Infinite Energy: The Secret to Never Feeling Drained

Lightning Focus: Mastering the Art of Productivity in a Distracted World

Saturnalia Manifestation Magick: A Guide to Unlocking Abundance During the Solstice

Graboids and Garland: The Ultimate Tremors-Themed Christmas Guide

12 Nights of Holiday Magic

The Power of Pause: 60-Second Mindfulness Practices

The Quick Reset: How to Reclaim Your Life After Burnout

The Shadow Eater: A Tale of Despair and Survival

The Micro-Mastery Method: Transform Your Skills in Just Minutes a Day

Reclaiming Time: How to Live More by Doing Less

Chronovore: The Eternal Nexus

The Mind Reset: Unlocking Your Inner Peace in a Chaotic World

Confidence Code: Building Unshakable Self-Belief

Baby the Vampire Terrier

Baby the Vampire Terrier's Christmas Adventure

Celestial Streams: The Content Creator's Astrology Manual

The Wealth Whisperer: Unlocking Abundance with Everyday Actions

The Energy Equation: Maximize Your Output Without Burning Out

The Happiness Algorithm: Science-Backed Steps to Joyful Living

Stress-Free Success: Achieving Goals Without Anxiety

Mindful Wealth: The New Blueprint for Financial Freedom

The Festive Flavors of New Year: A Culinary Celebration

The Master's Gambit: Keys of Eternal Power

Shadowed Secrets: Groundhog Day Mysteries

Beneath the Burrow: Lessons from the Groundhog

Spring's Whispers: The Groundhog's Prediction

If you want solar for your home go here: https://www.harborso-lar.live/apophisenterprises/

Get Some Tarot cards: https://www.makeplayingcards.com/sell/apophis-occult-shop

<u>Get some shirts: https://www.bonfire.com/store/apophis-shirt-emporium/</u>

<u>**Instagrams:**</u>
@apophis_enterprises,
@apophisbookemporium,
@apophisscardshop
Twitter: @apophisenterpr1
Tiktok:@apophisenterprise
Youtube: @sg1fan23477, @FiresideRetreatKingdom
Hive: @sg1fan23477
CheeLee: @SG1fan23477

Podcast: Apophis Chat Zone: https://open.spotify.com/show/5zXbrCLEV2xzCp8ybrfHsk?si=fb4d4fdbdce44dec

Newsletter: https://apophiss-newsletter-27c897.beehiiv.com/

If you want to support me or see posts of other projects that I have come over to: **buymeacoffee.com/mpetchinskg**
I post there daily several times a day

Get your Dinowicca or Christmas themed digital products, especially Santa Raptor songs and other musics. Here:
https://sg1fan23477.gumroad.com

Apophis Yuletide Digital has not only digital Christmas items, but it will have all things with Dinowicca as well as other Digital products.

www.ingramcontent.com/pod-product-compliance
Lightning Source LLC
Chambersburg PA
CBHW060912130726
48001CB00006B/2208